GUINNESS ILLUSTRATED COLLECTION
OF
WORLD RECORDS FOR YOUNG PEOPLE

Norris McWhirter and Ross McWhirter have been combing the world for twenty years collecting fantastic achievements, incredible stunts and bizarre marvels of nature for their GUINNESS BOOK OF WORLD RECORDS.

Now they've created a series especially for you! And each book in the GUINNESS ILLUSTRATED COLLECTION OF WORLD RECORDS FOR YOUNG PEOPLE comes with Norris McWhirter's and Ross McWhirter's personal guarantee that every achievement, fact or event recorded—no matter how unbelievable—is absolutely true!

David Ryder, a polio victim from Essex, England, left Los Angeles on March 30, 1970, and arrived in New York City 4½ months later on August 14, after covering 2,960 miles— on his crutches!

GUINNESS BOOK OF EXTRAORDINARY EXPLOITS

BY NORRIS McWHIRTER
& ROSS McWHIRTER

Illustrated by Kenneth Laager

GUINNESS BOOK OF EXTRAORDINARY EXPLOITS
A Bantam Book / published by arrangement with
Sterling Publishing Co., Inc.

PRINTING HISTORY
Sterling edition published October 1977
2nd printing... August 1978
3rd printing... May 1979
Bantam edition / February 1980

ISBN 0-553-13640-2

Published simultaneously in the United States and Canada

PRINTED IN THE UNITED STATES OF AMERICA

INTRODUCTION

People's extraordinary experiences can be more astounding than fiction and fantasy. After 20 years of combing the world for the most astounding feats and events for the GUINNESS BOOK OF WORLD RECORDS, I realize that some of the human exploits included in this book seem unbelievable.

I want to assure our readers, however, that every feat and event illustrated is true and accurate. You can believe every statement made, for we have checked and authenticated everything.

NORRIS McWHIRTER

No hurt peelings! Kathy Wafler, 17, of Rochester, New York, took an apple $18\frac{1}{2}$ inches around and peeled the longest single unbroken apple peel on record—172 feet 4 inches. It took her $11\frac{1}{2}$ hours in October, 1976.

Maurice and Maralyn Bailey survived $118\frac{1}{3}$ days at sea (almost 4 months!) in an inflatable dinghy that measured only $4\frac{1}{2}$ feet across. They drifted in the northeast Pacific from March 4 to June 30, 1973.

Geronimo! The largest airborne attack in history was launched by Anglo-American forces during World War II near Arnhem in the Netherlands on September 14, 1944. The attacking forces were made up of 34,000 men, using 2,800 airplanes and 1,600 gliders.

Sounds fishy, but in January, 1968, Donal Heatley fought with a fish for a record 32 hours 5 minutes off Tauranga, New Zealand. The 20-foot broadbill weighed about 1,500 pounds, and towed Heatley's 13-ton boat 50 miles before breaking the line and escaping.

Werner Erhard of San Francisco, California, mailed out 62,824 personal Christmas cards in December, 1975. You'll find this a difficult exploit to lick.

"I wanna hold your haaaaaand . . . !" The record number of participants in a connected free fall in skydiving is 29, by the "National Enquirer" Skydivers. They held hands in a giant circle for 3 seconds as they parachuted down over Zephyr Hill, Florida, in March, 1974.

Believing in the power of digestion, Jimmy Davenport of Lexington, Kentucky, choked down 20 two-ounce frankfurters in 3 minutes 33 seconds on March 3, 1976. To be quite frank with you, this is a tough act to swallow.

The Reverend Robert Marshall of the Birmingham Unitarian Church in Michigan, delivered the longest sermon on record—60 hours 31 minutes (an average of 6 hours per commandment)—from January 1 to 3, 1976.

It takes quite a while before Rabbi Barry Silberg of Milwaukee, Wisconsin, reaches the end of his rope. In May, 1976, he skipped rope 50,000 times without a break or fault in 5 hours 15 minutes.

Their business is going under. John J. Gruener and R. Neal Watson, both Americans, dove a record 437 feet with scubas off Freeport, Grand Bahamas, in October, 1968.

The best in snow jobs! Sixten Jernberg of Sweden has won the most Olympic gold medals in cross-country skiing—a total of 4, won in the 1956, 1960, and 1964 Olympics.

On December 7, 1966, Christopher Timms slid 7,500 feet down an ice face into a crevasse on New Zealand's 10,200-foot-high Mt. Elie de Beaumont—and lived! Timms' companion was killed, but this is the greatest recorded fall survived by a mountaineer.

The oldest authoress to have her book published was Mrs. Alice Pollock of Haslemere, Surrey, England. Her "Portrait of My Victorian Youth" was published in March, 1971, when she was 102 years and 8 months old.

Thomas Mogavero of Leroy, New York, bowled for 130 hours 50 minutes in Rochester, New York, October 22-28, 1975. He rolled 861 games using a 16-pound ball.

Rocky Marciano, heavyweight champ from 1952 to 1956, was still a hit when he quit the ring. He shares with Gene Tunney the honor of finally retiring as undefeated world heavyweight boxing champion.

Ray Stits designed and built the smallest airplane ever flown—the Stits "Skybaby" biplane. Nine feet 10 inches long, with a 7-foot 2-inch wing span and only 452 pounds in weight, this bug has a top speed of 185 m.p.h. A friend flew it in Riverside, California, in May, 1952.

Mrs. Mary E. Davis set the women's non-stop talking record of 110 hours 30 minutes 5 seconds. She started talking at a radio station in Buffalo, New York, on September 2, 1958, and did not stop until 5 days later in Tulsa, Oklahoma.

Sultan Selim III shot an arrow 1,400 Turkish "pikes" or "gez" near Istanbul, Turkey, in 1798. The distance is equal to somewhere between 953 and 972 yards.

They know how to face the music. Bill and Bobbie Irvine of London, England, are the world's most successful professional ballroom dancing champions. They won 13 world titles from 1960 to 1972.

Angelica Rozeanu of Rumania knows which way the ball bounces. She has won the most World Women's Singles titles in table tennis—a total of 6, from 1950 to 1955.

People thought they were full of hot air, but Pilâtre de Rosier and Marquis d'Arlandes flew the world's first manned balloon on November 21, 1783, near Paris, France. The hot-air balloon, which was built by Etienne Montgolfier, carried them 3,000 feet up in a 20-minute flight.

The fastest time in which anyone has successfully extracted the 23rd root of a 200-digit number by merely "thinking it out" is $10\frac{1}{2}$ minutes. Willem Klein of the Netherlands set this record in Lyon, France, on March 5, 1975. Would you call him a very calculating person?

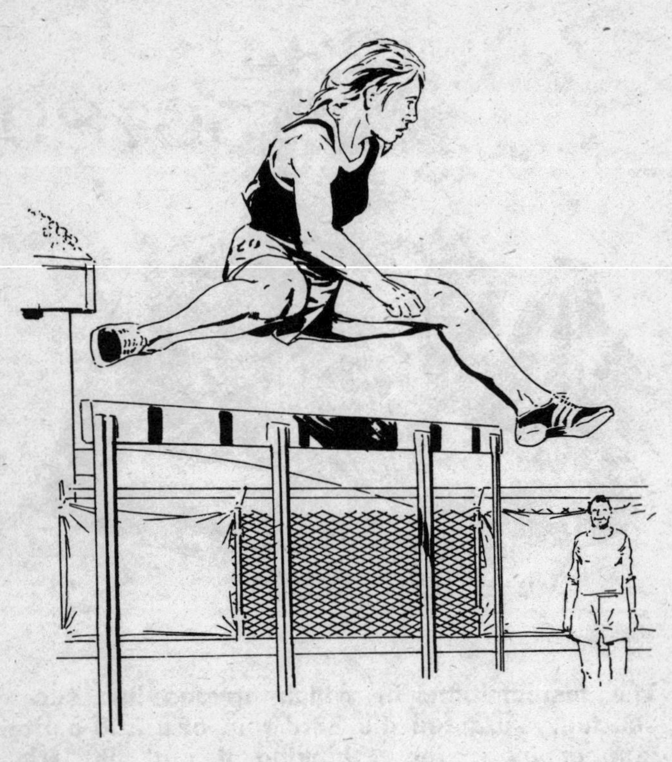

Overcoming all obstacles, Annelie Ehrhardt of East Germany set the women's 100-meter hurdling record of 12.59 seconds in Munich, West Germany, in September, 1972.

Tony Bellus squeezed his way into the record book by playing an electric accordion for 53 hours, December 11-13, 1975, at the Holiday Inn in Oakbrook Terrace, Illinois.

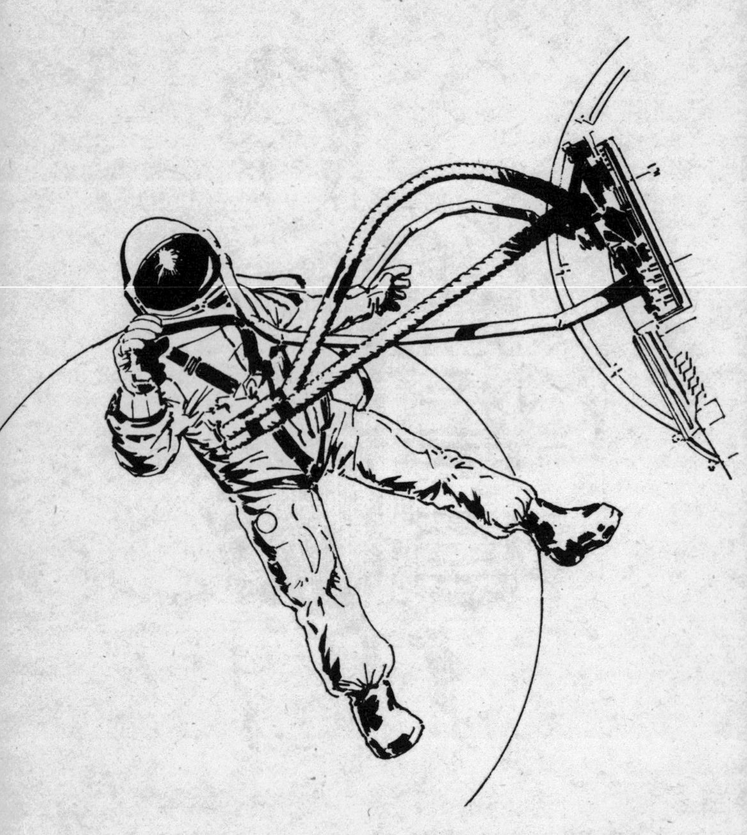

Here is an exploit that was out of this world! The first walk in space was made by Astronaut Edward H. White II, who floated outside his Gemini IV spacecraft for 21 minutes on June 3, 1965.

Have you ever tried to balance one golf ball on top of another? Mark Baumen of Grand Island, Nebraska, succeeded in balancing 5 new golf balls in this way without using any tape or glue in November, 1974. This feat was duplicated by Lang Martin of Charlotte, North Carolina in 1977.

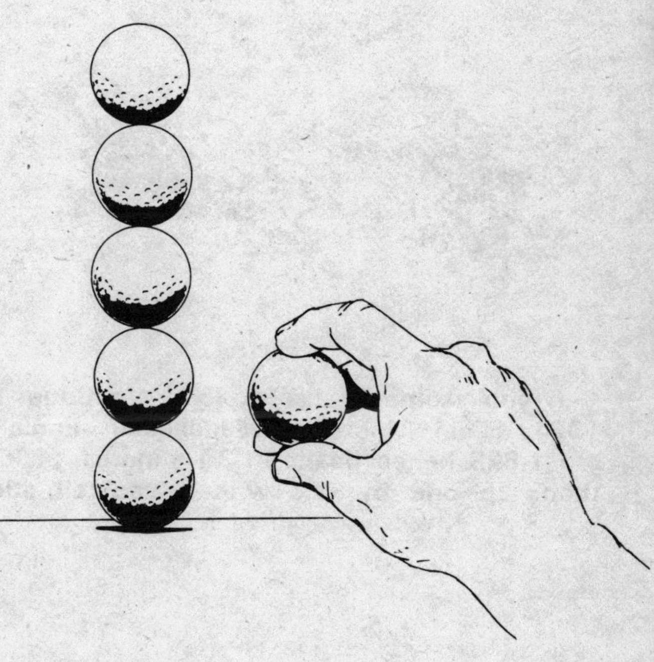

Can you stomach this exploit? On June 19, 1974, Nigel Moore of Manchester, England, ate 1,823 baked beans in 30 minutes, picking them up one by one with a cocktail stick.

Tom Sims is really a high roller. He cleared a high-jump bar set 4 feet $5\frac{1}{2}$ inches above the ground from a skateboard at the New York World Masters contest on June 19, 1976.

In April, 1974, Arden Chapman of Northeast Louisiana University, caught a grape thrown from a record distance of 204 feet—in his mouth!

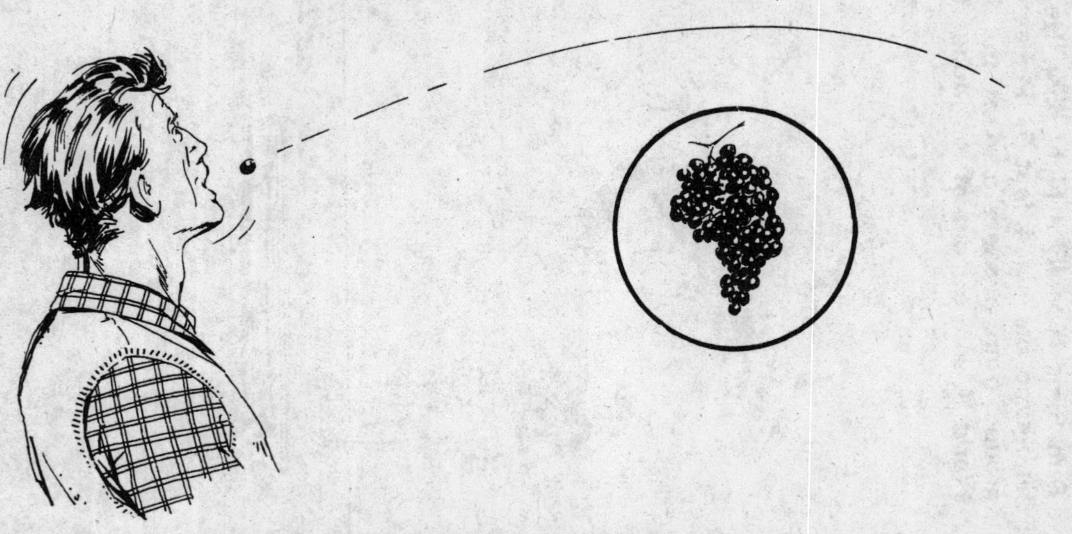

Not pressed for time, Mrs. J. Maassen won
the longest recorded ironing marathon, going
89 hours 32 minutes in Melbourne, Australia,
in March, 1973.

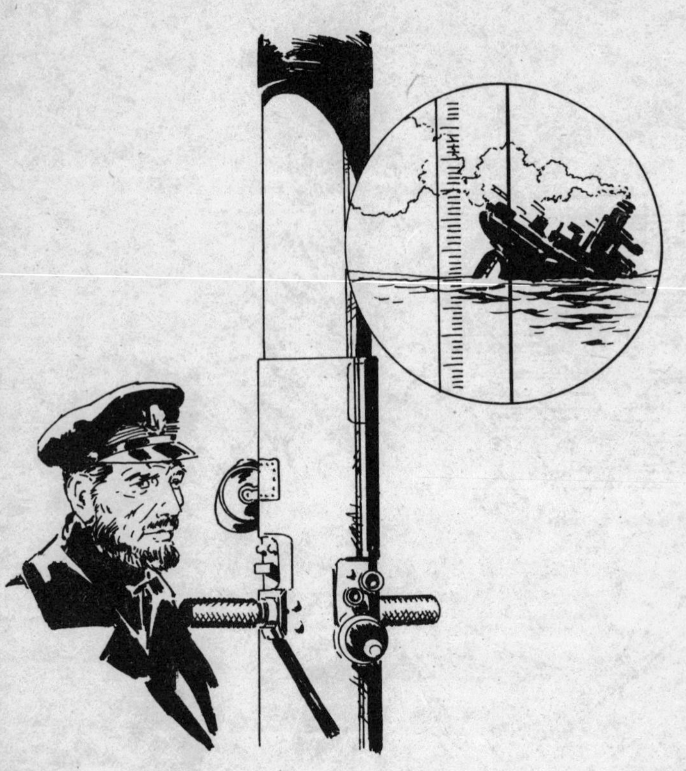

He torpedoed enemy ships and rose to the top. The deadliest of all World War II submarine commanders was Leutnant Herbert Schultze, captain of the German U.48, who sank one escort vessel and 51 allied merchant ships.

The top-selling novelist of all time is Erle Stanley Gardner, creator of that man of justice, Perry Mason. Before his death in 1970, Gardner's books sold more than 300 million copies in 23 languages. He sometimes worked with his staff on as many as seven novels—all at the same time!

He'll win any race hands down. Rick Sorrell of Franklin, Ohio, "ran" a 50-yard sprint on his hands in a record time of 24.2 seconds on July 1, 1975. Rick rarely goes down to "de-feet."

In 1657, Bernice Bardolf of Barnsley, Yorkshire, England, wrote down a recipe for a dish served at the Black Horse Tavern. In September, 1969, the recipe was found buried in the yard of the Alhambra Hotel in Barnsley, making it the oldest known surviving recipe. "Barnsley Bardolf," a version of the dish, is now on the hotel's menu—a perfect example of handing down traditions "by word of mouth."

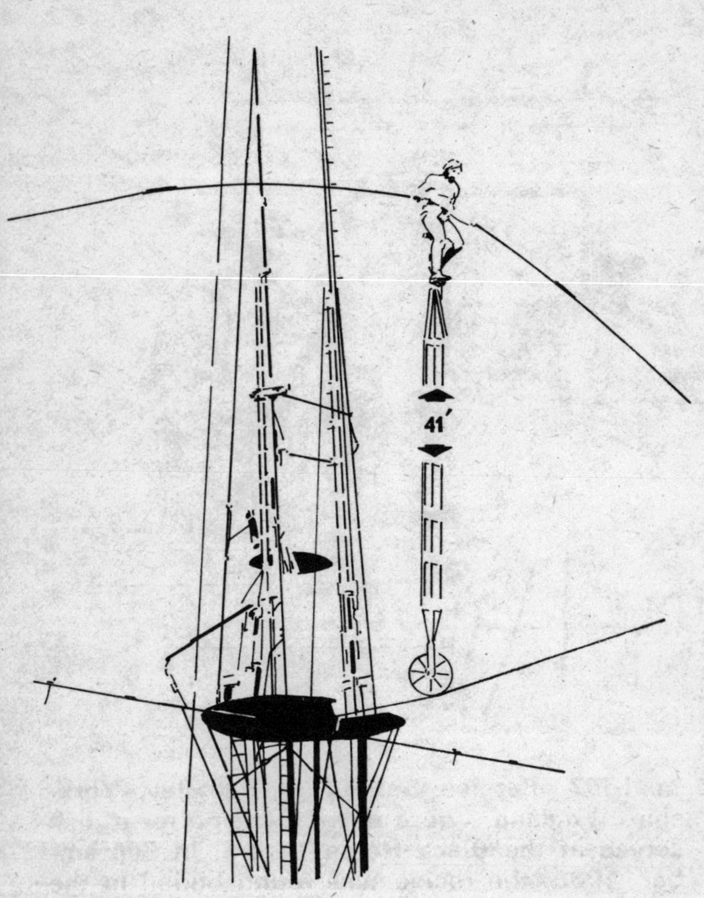

Steve McPeak of Las Vegas, Nevada, built and rode a unicycle 41 feet high—the highest on record. He set another record by riding this unique cycle on a 12-foot-long wire, 40 feet up in the air.

Many people have only one goal in life. Reggie Leach had 80 in one National Hockey League season, including the play-offs. Leach, a Philadelphia Flyer, lit up the scoreboard that many times in the 1975-1976 season.

The record speed for snowmobiles is 127.3 m.p.h. set by Yvon Duhamel of Canada on a Ski Doo XR-2 in February, 1973.

In 1911, two brothers, Temple and Louis Abernathy of Texas, then aged 9 and 11, rode 3,619 miles on horseback—the longest horseback ride on record. The trip from Coney Island in New York City to San Francisco took 62 days.

You're part of this exploit! The people of the United States drink more carbonated soft drinks than any other people—30.3 gallons per person (that's more than 160 bottles or cans) per year.

In countries where a man can have many wives, he can't always keep track of all his children. The last Sharifian Emperor of Morocco, Moulay Ismail, called "The Bloodthirsty" (1672-1727), was believed to have fathered a total of **548** sons and **340** daughters!

The world's record for rope quoit throwing is an unbroken sequence of 4,002 pegs by Bill Irby, Sr., of Australia in 1968. Quoit amazing!

Here's an easy way to write home. In sky-writing, a 7-letter word may stretch 6 miles long and can be seen from 50 miles away. Cyril Turner wrote the first sky-message over the Epsom racecourse in England on May 30, 1922. He spelled out "London Daily Mail" from a biplane.

Conrad Gerster peeled 39 pounds 10¾ ounces of onions in November, 1975, at the annual onion peeling contest in Bern, Switzerland. The contest itself has been described as a "tearful reonion."

A baseless claim to fame? Don Larsen of the New York Yankees did not allow a single Brooklyn Dodger to reach first base when he pitched the only perfect game ever seen in a World Series on October 8, 1956.

This movie had some teeth in it! The film that earned the highest world gross earnings is "Jaws." Let loose in June, 1975, it earned $124,000,000 in its first 78 days in North America alone.

Long a popular game among men, billiards has also been mastered by women. Maureen Baynton holds the record by winning 9 women's amateur world titles. She chalked them up between 1955 and 1968.

Of 100,010 pine blocks tossed, Tom Frye hit 100,004 in October, 1959, using a pair of automatic loading .22-caliber rifles.

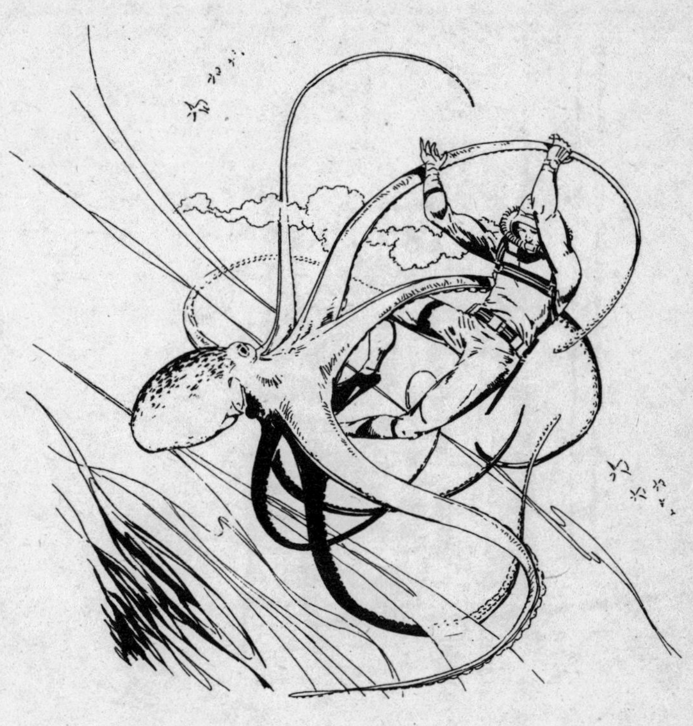

His opponent was well-armed, but skindiver Donald Hagen single-handedly wrestled a common Pacific octopus up from under Puget Sound, Washington, in February, 1973. It measured 25 feet 7 inches across and weighed 118 pounds.

Auguste and Louis Lumière gave the earliest demonstration of a cinematograph film in Paris on March 22, 1895. The film that started it all was called "La Sortie des Ouvriers de l'Usine Lumière." Understand?

The $ound of music. The most commercially successful of all song writers have been John Lennon and Paul McCartney, formerly of the Beatles. Between 1962 and 1970 they wrote 30 songs which sold more than 1,000,000 records each!

Irena Rodnina has won a record total of 8 world pairs titles in figure skating, four of them with her husband, Aleksandr Zaitsev. This same pair was also awarded a record 11 perfect marks for a performance in 1974.

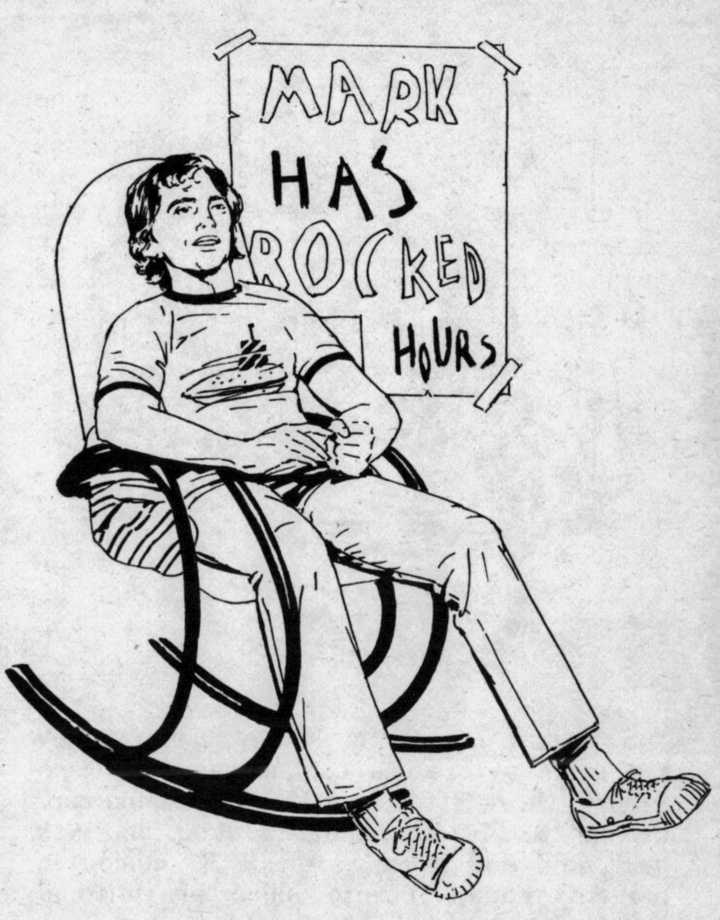

Some thought he was off his rocker. Actually, Mark Pauga was *on* it—for 336 hours! Mark took a rocking route into the record book by establishing the longest duration ever for a rocking chair "Rockathon" from July 27 to August 10, 1975, in Lombard, Illinois.

The biggest ransom in history was paid by the Incas to Spanish conquistador Francisco Pizarro. He held the Inca chief Atahualpa captive in 1532-33 at Cajamarca, Peru, and was paid gold and silver worth $170 million in modern money. Pizarro killed his prisoner anyway.

The record Trans-Canada (Halifax to Vancouver) walk of 3,764 miles is 94 days by Clyde McRae. Clyde accomplished this "sole-itary" feat from May 1 to August 4, 1973.

The longest banana split of all time was served by Farrell's Ice Cream Parlour Restaurant in St. Paul, Minnesota, in January, 1973. A mile long, it was made up of 10,580 bananas and 33,000 scoops of ice cream. Naturally, the crowd of onlookers went bananas before splitting.

On July 29, 1956, Capt. Jacques-Yves Cousteau anchored his research vessel "Calypso" in the mid-Atlantic Romanche Trench. He needed a 5½-mile-long nylon cable line to do it, since this was the deepest anchorage ever achieved —24,600 feet!

The annual Housewives Pancake Race, which originated in Olney, England, is also held in the United States. Kathleen West created quite a flap when she battered the record for the winding 415-yard course in Liberal, Kansas, finishing on top of the stack in 59.1 seconds in February, 1970.

The smallest bicycle in the world, with $2\frac{1}{8}$-inch wheels and weighing 2 pounds, was built by Charlie Charles, who rides it at the Circus Circus Hotel in Las Vegas, Nevada. Charlie set another record in 1976 by staying motionless on a bicycle for 7 hours.

Champion boxer Jack Broughton put some punch into the rules when he drew up the earliest prize-ring code in England on August 16, 1743. Broughton was champ from 1729 to 1750.

The marathon record for choir singing is 40 hours, set by the Cleveland High School choir of Seattle, Washington, April 9-11, 1976.

Only three people have won world championships in water skiing twice—Alfredo Mendoza (U.S.) in 1953 and 1955; Mike Suyderhoud (U.S.) in 1967 and 1969; and George Athans (Canada) in 1971 and 1973.

Stair a doctor in the house? On February 27, 1972, Dr. Randolph W. Seed set a stair-climbing record by conquering 100 stories of the John Hancock Building in Chicago, Illinois, in 14 minutes 29 seconds.

The earliest trip around the world was made under the command of Juan Sebastian de Elcano. Of the 5 original ships in Magellan's expedition, only the "Vittoria," under de Elcano's command, survived the 30,700-mile voyage. It returned to San Lucur, Spain, on September 6, 1521, having been away for 2 years.

In July, 1920, Hermann Görner made a one-handed dead lift of $734\frac{1}{2}$ pounds. His other weighty accomplishments included raising 24 men weighing 4,123 pounds on a plank with the soles of his feet, and carrying a 1,444-pound piano on his back for a distance of $52\frac{1}{2}$ feet.

Taking all his properties together, it seems oil giant Jean Paul Getty's wealth was the largest on earth. Getty's riches totaled more than $1,750,000,000 when he died in 1976.

Pelé the soccer king has for the greater part
of his 20-year career averaged a goal a game.
His total before he came to play in the
United States in 1975 was 1,216!

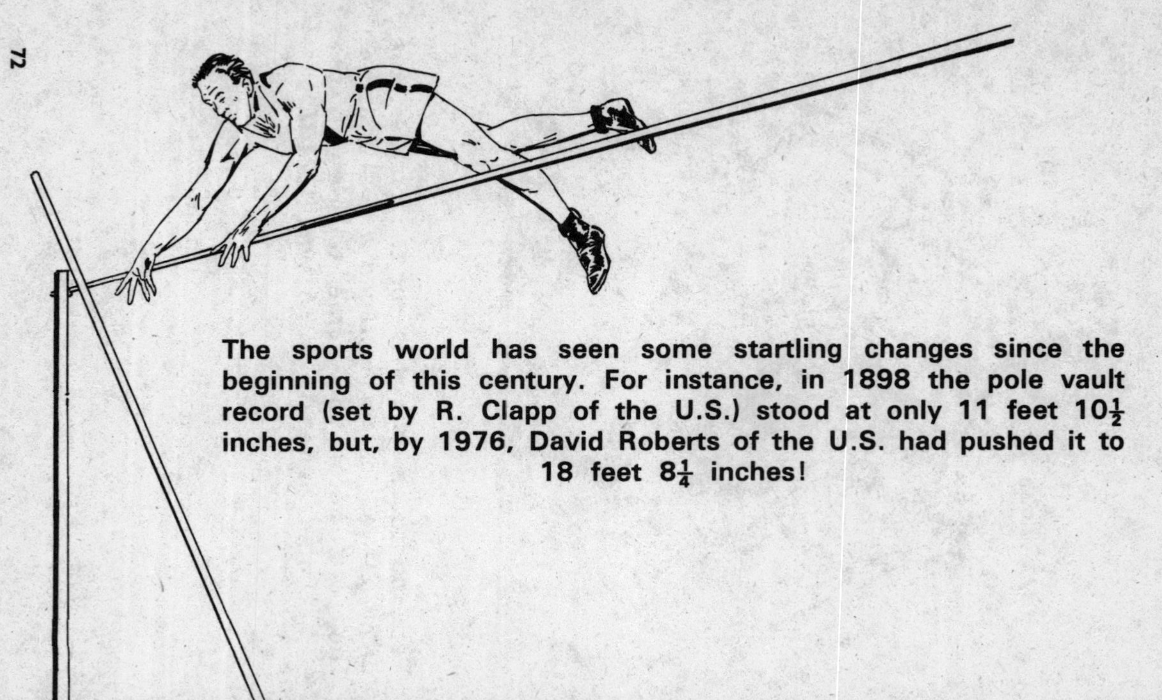

The sports world has seen some startling changes since the beginning of this century. For instance, in 1898 the pole vault record (set by R. Clapp of the U.S.) stood at only 11 feet $10\frac{1}{2}$ inches, but, by 1976, David Roberts of the U.S. had pushed it to 18 feet $8\frac{1}{4}$ inches!

Lt. Col. Valentina Tereshkova really went
around in circles when she became the first
woman to orbit the earth! She completed
48 orbits in "Vostok VI" on June 16, 1963.

Otto E. Funk walked 4,165 miles from New York City to San Francisco, playing a violin every step of the way. He finished the trip on June 16, 1929, after 183 days on the road, so becoming the original Fiddler on the Hoof.

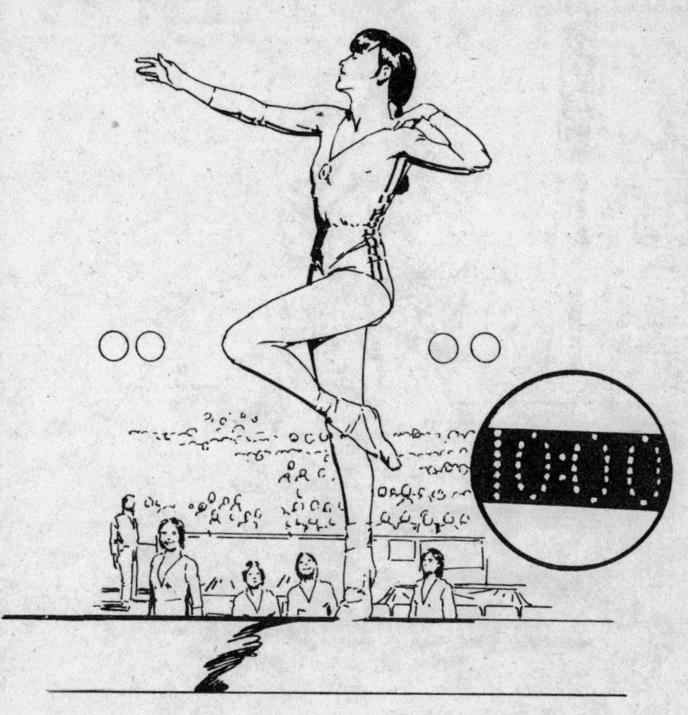

She's Nadia just another pretty face! Nadia Comaneci of Rumania became the first gymnast in Olympic history to win a perfect score of 10.00. She finished the 1976 Olympics in Montreal with seven such perfect scores!

In 1972, Frank Jones of Lowestoft, Suffolk, England, finally caught up with his brother, Arthur Jones. He had been searching for him since 1904—for 68 years!

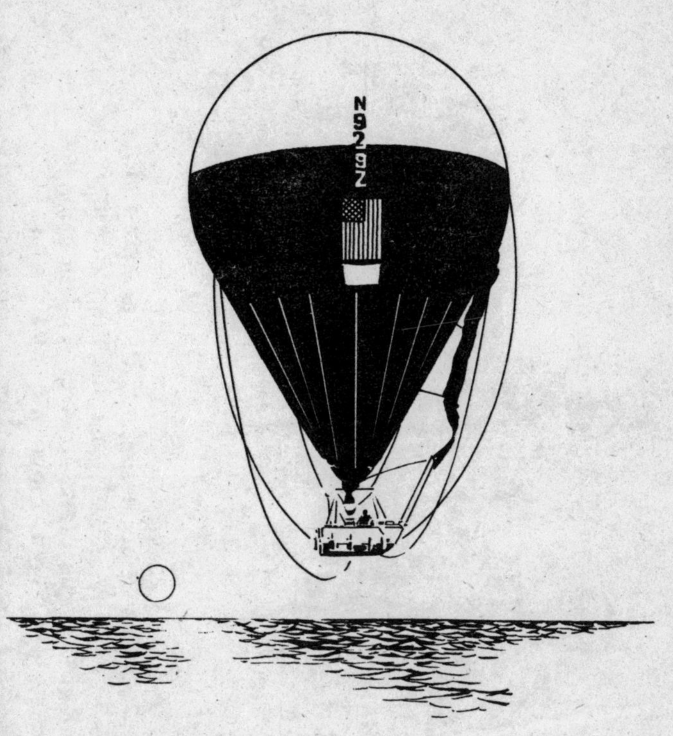

The longest manned balloon flight was by Ed Yost, who stayed airborne for 107 hours 37 minutes, covering 2,740 miles. Yost lifted off from Milbridge, Maine, October 5, 1976, and touched down at sea 200 miles east of the Azores 5 days later.

Jude Acers took on 179 chess opponents all at the same time in Hicksville, New York, in July, 1976—the greatest number of opponents ever tackled in a single start. He won 160 games, lost 15 and drew 4 in 19 hours. Your move sir, sir, sir, sir . . .

Dr. Allan V. Abbott of San Bernardino, California, achieved the highest speed ever on a bicycle—140.5 m.p.h.! He pedaled behind a windshield mounted on a car at the Bonneville Salt Flats, Utah, in August, 1973.

In archery, the greatest number of world titles ever won by a man is four, strung together by H. Deutgen of Sweden in 1947, 1948, 1949, and 1950. Take a bow, Mr. Deutgen!

This is really far out! On February 15, 1913, the ship "Fram" sailed to latitude 78° 41′ S. off the Antarctic coast—the farthest point south ever reached by a ship!

The smallest breed of horse is raised by Julio Falabella of Argentina. Grown-ups range from under 18 to 30 inches at the shoulder and weigh only 40 to 80 pounds.

Aside from his other achievements, Thomas Alva Edison (1847-1931) also built the first successful phonograph. He got his first patent on February 19, 1878, for a machine constructed by his mechanic, John Kryesi.

Success was just a stone's throw away from Warren Klope, who topped a 1975 stone-skipping contest in Troy, Michigan, with a record 24 skips.

Strokes of genius! In 1961, Mihir Sen of India swam across 4 major waterways—from India to Ceylon, the Dardanelles, the Straits of Gibraltar, and the length of the Panama Canal!

Terry Lemus performs a difficult triple back somersault with $1\frac{1}{2}$ twists in her trapeze act at the Circus Circus Hotel in Las Vegas, Nevada. She first performed this feat in 1969.

Bernd Kannenberg of West Germany takes things in stride. He holds 4 world records for track walking set in 1974 and 1975.

A towiffic idea! In 1927, Frank J. Elliott and George A. Scott of Nova Scotia, persuaded 168 passing motorists to tow their engineless Model T Ford for 4,759 miles. They covered the distance in 89 days to win a $1,000 bet.

The most famous of all escape artists was Ehrich Weiss, who called himself Harry Houdini (1874-1926). Houdini pioneered underwater escapes from locked, roped, and weighted containers while handcuffed and shackled with irons. His name, however, will never escape anyone's memory.

Al Oerter of the U.S. won the discus competition in 4 Olympic meetings, one after the other, from 1956 to 1968. This is a unique achievement in Olympic track and field that needs no further discussion.

Plennie Wingo had plenty of time, so he walked from Santa Monica, California, to Istanbul, Turkey, a distance of 8,000 miles—backwards! Using special glasses to see where he was going, he went thataway from April, 1931, to October, 1932.

Barney Quinn of Ottawa, Canada, made the longest recorded throw in lacrosse history in September, 1892—162.86 yards!

In surfing, the highest waves usually are about 30 or 35 feet tall. However, the highest wave ever ridden was a "tsunami" or tidal wave of "perhaps 50 feet," which struck Minole, Hawaii, on April 3, 1868. With unwavering courage, a Hawaiian named Holua rode it to save his life.

Y. A. Tittle of the New York Giants, always seemed to make good connections. One of football's all-time great quarterbacks, Tittle threw a record 36 touchdown passes in 1963 and 7 in one game in 1962. (Both marks have been equaled by other quarterbacks but never beaten.)

She's got a rich voice and a wealth of talent. Liza Minnelli was paid the highest night-club fee in history—$100,000 for one New Year's Eve in 1975. Patrons paid $150 per seat to watch her.

INDEX